Monday	10 a.m. - 9 p.m.
Tuesday	10 a.m. - 9 p.m.
Wednesday	1 p.m. - 9 p.m.
Thursday	10 a.m. - 9 p.m.
Friday	10 a.m. - 5 p.m.
Saturday	10 a.m. - 5 p.m.
Sunday	1 p.m. - 5 p.m.

COOKING THE LEBANESE WAY

Lerner Publications Company
A division of Lerner Publishing Group
241 First Avenue North
Minneapolis, MN 55401 U.S.A.

Website address: www.lernerbooks.com

Library of Congress Cataloging-in-Publication Data

Amari, Suad.
Cooking the Lebanese way / by Suad Amari—Rev. and expanded.
p. cm. — (Easy menu ethnic cookbooks)
Includes index.
Summary: An introduction to the cooking of Lebanon featuring such traditional recipes as kabobs, hummus, chard and yogurt soup, and bulgur pilaf. Also includes information on the history, geography, customs and people of this Middle Eastern country.
ISBN: 0–8225–4116–5 (lib. bdg. : alk. paper)
1. Cookery, Lebanese—Juvenile literature. 2. Lebanon—Social life and customs—Juvenile literature. [1. Cookery, Lebanese. 2. Lebanon—Social life and customs.] I. Title. II. Series.
TX725.L4 A43 2003
641.595692—dc21 2001007211

Manufactured in the United States of America
1 2 3 4 5 6 – JR – 08 07 06 05 04 03

easy menu ethnic cookbooks

COOKING THE LEBANESE WAY

revised and expanded to include new low-fat and vegetarian recipes

Suad Amari

Lerner Publications Company • Minneapolis

Contents

Introduction

Foods with international origins—such as pasta, stir-fries, and tacos—frequently appear on menus in the United States alongside hamburgers and French fries. For many years, however, tabbouleh, hummus, and other foods of the Middle East were not very common outside of their native region.

Fortunately for diners in the rest of the world, the popularity and availability of this delicious cuisine have grown greatly. Cooks in the United States have discovered that the Middle Eastern diet, with its emphasis on using fruits, vegetables, and grains, is as delicious as it is healthy and versatile. Lebanon, a country in the very heart of the Middle East, is especially famous for its cuisine, which represents all that is best in the cooking of this historic region.

Savory garlic chicken with fresh fruit on the side makes a satisfying evening meal. (Recipe on page 52.)

The Land

Lebanon, the smallest country in the Middle East, is only about 30 miles wide and 135 miles long. It is bounded on the west by the Mediterranean Sea. On the north, east, and south, the tiny country is hemmed in by its larger neighbors Syria and Israel.

The landscape of Lebanon is rugged, with two parallel mountain ranges, the Lebanon and the Anti-Lebanon Mountains, running the length of the country. The Bekáa Valley lies between these mountains. Much of this fertile region is watered by the Litani River, which flows southward and then westward to the Mediterranean Sea. A narrow plain runs along the Mediterranean coast, and most of Lebanon's cities are located in this coastal region, including Beirut (the national capital) and the major cities of Tripoli and Sidon.

Although the amount of cropland in Lebanon is limited, the country is able to produce almost all of its own food. Lebanese farmers make the most of available land by cutting flat fields (terraces) into the steep hillsides and mountain slopes. And, thanks to abundant winter rainfall, there is plenty of water for thirsty crops.

Lebanese crops also get plenty of sun. Like most Mediterranean countries, Lebanon generally enjoys warm temperatures. However, its diverse terrain also gives this small nation a wide range of climates. Summers in Beirut can get quite hot, but many people are able to escape the heat by visiting the snow-covered mountains nearby. Lebanon is the only country in the Middle East where skiing is a major sport, and people can easily ski in the mountains and swim in the warm waters of the Mediterranean on the same day!

The History

Because of its geographical position at the crossroads of the Middle East, Lebanon's long history is also very complex. For centuries, Lebanon was ruled by foreign powers, and it only became an independent country in the 1940s.

In ancient times, the stretch of land that would one day become Lebanon was part of a country called Phoenicia. Phoenicia was conquered by the Greek military leader Alexander the Great in 332 B.C. Nearly three hundred years later, the region came under the control of the vast Roman Empire. During the long period of Roman rule, many people of the area became Christians. In the A.D. 600s, a new religious force, Islam, swept through the Middle East. Islam is a religion that was founded by the prophet Muhammad on the Arabian Peninsula. The followers of Islam, called Muslims, took control of the eastern Mediterranean region, including the territory known to Christians as the Holy Land.

In this illustration of a battle, European Christians (left) and Middle Eastern Muslims (right) clash in the struggle for control of the Holy Land, which includes parts of present-day Lebanon.

During the 1100s and 1200s, armies of Christian soldiers from Europe invaded the Middle East, seeking to capture the Holy Land. After a long and bloody series of wars called the Crusades, Muslim forces were victorious over the Christian armies. Although many of Lebanon's inhabitants remained Christian, the region once again became part of the Islamic world. From 1516 to 1918, the country was ruled by the Ottoman Turks as a part of the province of Syria. After the Ottoman Empire was defeated in World War I (1914–1918), Lebanon was placed under French control. In 1941 Lebanon formally won its independence from France, but the turbulent transition lasted until 1943. The Lebanese commemorate November 22, 1943, as their national Independence Day.

But independence did not bring peace and prosperity to Lebanon. The country continued to be a battleground for other warring nations of the Middle East, and beginning in the late 1960s Lebanon endured invasions and attacks related to conflicts between Israelis and Palestinians in neighboring regions. By the mid-1970s, Lebanon was also plagued by civil war, with groups of Lebanese fighting each other in the streets of Beirut.

Some of this strife is due to Lebanon's location in the midst of a turbulent part of the world. Other problems are caused by religious differences within the country. Most Lebanese are Muslims, belonging to one of three different sects: Sunni, Shiite, or Druze. But Lebanon is also home to a large Christian population. Almost one-quarter of its citizens are members of the Maronite Church, a division of the Roman Catholic Church. Other Christians in Lebanon include followers of Greek Orthodoxy, Roman Catholicism, and Protestantism. Lebanon is the only Arab country in the world with such a diversity of Muslims and Christians, and disagreements among these many religious groups have been a source of serious conflict.

During the late 1980s and early 1990s, the civil war drew to a close and a tentative peace was restored to Lebanon through a series of cease-fires and treaties. However, violence related to international conflicts continued to trouble the country, and at the beginning of the 2000s Lebanon and its people are still hoping for lasting calm.

Even as Lebanon suffered through the devastation of a long internal war, the Lebanese people maintained many but not all of the traditions of their old way of life. Afterward, as the country began to recover and rebuild, people gradually returned to the customs that they had abandoned. Many of these time-honored habits have to do with the preparation and enjoyment of food. The markets of modern-day Beirut display a wide range of fresh fruits and vegetables for sale. Cafés and restaurants offer diners a delicious assortment of *mezze* dishes, the appetizers for which Lebanese cooking is famous. After all that their nation has been through, the Lebanese people continue to enjoy the simple pleasure of a good meal with family and friends.

Holidays and Festivals

Lebanon's unique blend of Muslim and Christian populations results in a local abundance of religious holidays. From Eid al-Fitr to Easter, festivities of all sorts involve friends, family, and lots of delicious food.

The Islamic holy month of Ramadan is one of the most important holiday seasons of the year for Muslims. Ramadan commemorates Allah (God) giving the Quran, the holy book of Islam, to the prophet Muhammad, and the month is a time for fasting and prayer. Most adult Muslims neither eat nor drink from sunup to sundown during this month. Before dawn, a light breakfast such as milk, fruit, and a sandwich of *labneh* (a Middle Eastern cheese made with yogurt) is eaten. During the day, Lebanese Muslims visit mosques (Muslim places of worship) to pray and to attend special holiday services. After dark another meal, called the *iftar,* is eaten. In Lebanon the iftar is usually a festive affair, and family and friends often gather to enjoy breaking the day's fast. The nighttime streets are lit with strings of lights, and some neighborhoods set up tents in which people meet to play cards, sing songs, and, of course, to eat. The first bite of food is traditionally a snack of dates, often accompanied by

Holiday sweets and other treats fill the shelves of this Lebanese pastry shop.

a sweet drink of some kind. A variety of delicious Lebanese classics may follow this light start, and soups are a traditional favorite. Local shops sell tempting sweets, and many families splurge on special desserts for their Ramadan suppers.

At the end of Ramadan, Muslims celebrate with the great feast of Eid al-Fitr. This holiday lasts for three or four days and gives everyone a chance to rejoice and to reflect on the past month. Most Lebanese families give their homes a thorough cleaning and go shopping for new clothes. Children get to celebrate with gifts and toys, and young and old celebrate with magnificent meals that last into the night.

Another very important holiday for Lebanese Muslims is Eid al-Adha, or the Feast of the Sacrifice. Eid al-Adha falls during the hajj, the annual pilgrimage to the holy city of Mecca in Saudi Arabia. Every Muslim must try to make the hajj once during his or her lifetime, and the festival celebrates the journey of the pilgrims. Eid al-Adha also celebrates a story in the Quran in which a father is willing to sacrifice his son for Allah but is stopped and rewarded for his faith. To commemorate this story, Muslim families traditionally roast a lamb, sharing the meat with friends, neighbors, and the poor. Those who cannot afford such a feast often enjoy a meat stew. Like Eid al-Fitr, the festivities of Eid al-Adha usually last for three or four days and include special visits to mosques, gifts of clothes and toys, and many family gatherings and meals.

Lebanese Christians, like Christians around the world, observe Easter and Christmas as the two most important religious holidays of the year. Holy Week and Easter in Lebanon are marked by parades, beginning on Palm Sunday (the Sunday before Easter), when children and their families carry palm leaves, flowers, and candles through the streets. Local priests begin the Easter Sunday celebration well before dawn, leading midnight processions to dark and quiet churches. The priest knocks on the doors of the church and demands to enter. He is refused twice by a mysterious voice (usually a congregation member who is waiting inside the building). The third time the priest knocks, the doors are thrown open, the lights come on, and the congregation enters to begin celebrating Easter Sunday. After church services, families and friends visit with each other and share a great feast. And no Lebanese Easter would be complete without *maamoul*, a sweet pastry filled with dates or nuts.

Christmas is another big event in Lebanon, and the streets of cities and towns are filled with festive lights and music. Crowds of shoppers purchase gifts, decorations, and food at bustling bazaars and markets. A traditional Lebanese dance, called the *dabkeh*, is performed during the holiday season by people dressed in traditional clothing. In downtown Beirut, a Christmas tree that may be as tall as sixty-five feet towers over the central public square. Many families plant food seeds—such as beans, lentils, or grains—a few weeks before Christmas. With daily watering, these little plants grow several inches tall by Christmastime, when they are used to decorate the household nativity (figurines arranged to resemble the manger scene of Jesus' birth).

On Christmas Eve and Christmas Day, Lebanese Christians attend church services and pay each other visits. This time of year is popular for joyous reunions of family and friends. The biggest meal of the holiday is usually eaten on Christmas afternoon. Some households serve roast turkey for this midday feast, while others fill their tables

Workers finish decorating Beirut's public Christmas tree.

with more traditional Lebanese dishes, from *kibbeh* (spiced ground meat mixed with bulgur, a wheat product) to chicken and rice. A variety of sweets, including pastries, cookies, and traditional sugar-coated almonds, are enjoyed as snacks and desserts throughout the holiday season.

Secular, or nonreligious, celebrations in Lebanon include New Year's Eve and New Year's Day, marked by parties, feasts, dancing, and games. Independence Day, on November 22, commemorates the end of French control over Lebanon and features parades and public festivities. In addition to these national holidays, towns and villages all over the country hold festivals and feast days, some honoring religious figures such as patron saints (saints with special meaning to particular cities).

Music and art festivals also have a long history in Lebanon, and the largest of these is held in the ancient city of Baalbek. Begun in 1956, the Baalbek International Festival features performances by musicians, dancers, and actors from around the world and takes place amid dramatic Roman ruins. Like many Lebanese celebrations, the festival was not held during the civil war. But with returning peace, the Lebanese people are celebrating the festival once again with good music, good company, and good food.

At the Souk

Shoppers strolling down fashionable Hamra Street in Beirut may pass expensive shops and sidewalk cafés that resemble those in European cities. However, like the inhabitants of many other Middle Eastern countries, the Lebanese still do most of their shopping in street markets, called *souks* in Arabic. A souk consists of stalls and

Fresh produce is readily available to shoppers at their local souk.

shops with their fronts open to the street. When closed, the shops are completely covered by wooden or metal shutters.

In the souks of Lebanon, traders in particular kinds of goods are grouped together. There is the street of the spice sellers and perfume sellers, the street of the quiltmakers, and so on. In Beirut a huge covered market is reserved just for jewelry and precious metals.

The most colorful parts of the souk, however, are those that sell foods of all kinds. In the fruit and vegetable section of the market, shoppers inspect heaps of eggplants, tomatoes, onions, garlic, and fresh herbs such as mint, marjoram, and basil. Various kinds of greens are also available, including spinach, silverbeet, and the dark green leaves of *meloukhia*, a Middle Eastern plant that tastes somewhat like spinach. Spice sellers display huge gunnysacks of brown cumin and coriander seeds, red pepper, and golden turmeric and saffron.

The meat market, separate from the fruit and vegetable section, is another busy section of the souk. Mutton (sheep) and lamb are the main types of red meat sold in Lebanon. Beef and pork are rarely available. The mountainous countryside is not suitable for raising beef cattle, and pork is forbidden to Muslims and is not very popular with Lebanese Christians. However, all kinds of poultry are sold in the market, as well as rabbits and occasionally wild game such as venison (deer meat) or partridge. Souks in coastal towns offer a wide variety of fresh fish and seafood.

Shopping in the souk can be an exhausting business, especially in the summer. After finishing their errands, many shoppers refresh themselves with cooling drinks sold by street vendors. Lemonade, made from fresh, locally grown lemons and served ice cold, is very popular. Lebanese ice cream is another common summer cooler, and street vendors sell an enormous variety of fresh fruit flavors.

Cooks in Lebanon use their fresh purchases from the souk to prepare delicious and distinctive dishes. Even if you can't visit a Lebanese souk yourself, you can use the recipes in this book to begin cooking the Lebanese way and to get a taste of this unique cuisine.

Before You Begin

Lebanese recipes call for some ingredients that you may not know. Sometimes special cookware is used, too, although the recipes in this book can easily be prepared with ordinary utensils and pans.

The most important thing you need to know before you start is how to be a careful cook. On the following page, you'll find a few rules that will make your cooking experience safe, fun, and easy. Next, take a look at the "dictionary" of utensils, terms, and special ingredients. You may also want to read the section on preparing healthy, low-fat meals.

When you've picked out a recipe to try, read through it from beginning to end. Now you are ready to shop for ingredients and to organize the cookware you will need. Once you have assembled everything, you're ready to begin cooking.

Bite-sized pieces of toasted pita bread add crunch to this peasant salad. (Recipe on page 36.)

The Careful Cook

Whenever you cook, there are certain safety rules you must always keep in mind. Even experienced cooks follow these rules when they are in the kitchen.

- Always wash your hands before handling food. Thoroughly wash all raw vegetables and fruits to remove dirt, chemicals, and insecticides. Wash uncooked poultry, meats, and fish under cold water.
- Use a cutting board when cutting up vegetables and fruits. Don't cut them up in your hand! And be sure to cut in a direction *away* from you and your fingers.
- Long hair or loose clothing can easily catch fire if brought near the burners of a stove. If you have long hair, tie it back before you start cooking.
- Turn all pot handles toward the back of the stove so that you will not catch your sleeves or jewelry on them. This is especially important when younger brothers and sisters are around. They could easily knock off a pot and get burned.
- Always use a pot holder to steady hot pots or to take pans out of the oven. Don't use a wet cloth on a hot pan because the steam it produces could burn you.
- Lift the lid of a steaming pot with the opening away from you so that you will not get burned.
- If you get burned, hold the burn under cold running water. Do not put grease or butter on it. Cold water helps to take the heat out, but grease or butter will only keep it in.
- If grease or cooking oil catches fire, throw baking soda or salt at the bottom of the flame to put it out. (Water will *not* put out a grease fire.) Call for help, and try to turn all the stove burners to "off."

Cooking Utensils

colander—A bowl-shaped dish with holes in it that is used for washing or draining food

Dutch oven—A heavy pot with a tight-fitting domed lid that is often used for cooking soups or stews

potato masher—A utensil with a flat surface for mashing potatoes or other foods

sieve—A bowl-shaped device with very small holes or fine netting used for draining food or separating small particles from larger pieces of food

skewer—A thin wooden or metal rod used to hold small pieces of food for broiling or grilling

slotted spoon—A spoon with small openings in the bowl, used to remove solid food from a liquid

whisk—A wire utensil used for beating food by hand

Cooking Terms

baste—To pour, brush, or spoon liquid over food as it cooks in order to flavor and moisten it

boil—To heat a liquid over high heat until bubbles form and rise rapidly to the surface

broil—To cook food directly under a heat source so that the side facing the heat cooks rapidly

brown—To cook food quickly in fat over high heat so that the surface turns an even brown

garnish—To decorate a dish with small pieces of food, such as chopped parsley

knead—To work dough or another thick mixture by pressing it with the palms, pushing it outward and then pressing it over on itself

preheat—To allow an oven to warm up to a certain temperature before putting food in it

sauté—To fry quickly over high heat in oil or fat, stirring or turning the food to prevent burning

score—To make light cuts on the surface of food without cutting all the way through the food

simmer—To cook over low heat in liquid kept just below its boiling point

Special Ingredients

allspice—The berry of a West Indian tree, used whole or ground. The flavor of allspice resembles a combination of cinnamon, nutmeg, and cloves.

aniseed—The seed of the anise herb, which gives food a strong, aromatic flavor similar to that of black licorice. Aniseed is also called anise seed.

bulgur—Kernels of wheat that have been steamed, dried, and crushed. Bulgur is a staple food in the Middle East. A very similar product called cracked wheat may be used as a substitute for bulgur.

caraway seed—The whole seeds of an herb of the parsley family, used to flavor foods

cardamom seed—A spice of the ginger family, used whole or ground, that has a rich aroma and gives food a sweet, cool taste

cayenne pepper—Dried red chilies (hot peppers) ground to a fine powder

chard—A leafy green plant of the beet family

chickpeas—A type of pea with a nutlike flavor. Chickpeas are also called garbanzo beans and are available dried or canned.

converted rice—Rice that has been treated to preserve much of its nutritional value and that is fluffy when cooked

coriander—An herb used ground as a flavoring or fresh as a garnish. Fresh coriander is also known as cilantro.

cumin—The ground seeds of an herb in the parsley family, used in cooking to give food a slightly hot flavor

field bean—A variety of white bean native to the Middle East. Often called Egyptian field beans, they are available at Middle Eastern stores, specialty stores, and some supermarkets.

garlic—An herb whose distinctive flavor is used in many dishes. Each piece or bulb can be broken up into several smaller sections called cloves. Before chopping a clove of garlic, remove its papery skin.

ground ginger—A tangy, aromatic spice made from the underground stem of the ginger plant

ground rice—Rice that has been ground to a fine, flourlike consistency

hummus—A thick paste made of ground chickpeas, spices, and ground sesame seeds

mint—The leaves of any of a variety of mint plants, used fresh or dried in cooking

olive oil—An oil made from pressed olives that is used in cooking and for dressing salads

orange flower water—A flavoring made from distilled orange blossoms

pine nuts—The edible seeds of certain pine trees

pita bread—Flat, round loaves of bread common throughout the Middle East. When baked, a puffed pocket of air forms in the center of the bread.

rose water–A strong, sweet flavoring distilled from rose petals and used in many Middle Eastern dishes

scallions—A variety of green onion

tahini—A paste of ground sesame seeds

yeast—An ingredient used in baking that causes dough to rise and become light and fluffy. Yeast is available in either small, white cakes called compressed yeast or in granular form called active dry yeast.

zaatar—A mixture of wild thyme, sesame seeds, Lebanese sumac seeds, and salt

Healthy and Low-Fat Cooking Tips

Many modern cooks are concerned about preparing healthy, low-fat meals. Fortunately, there are simple ways to reduce the fat content of most dishes. Here are a few general tips for adapting the recipes in this book. Throughout the book, you'll also find specific suggestions for individual recipes—and don't worry, they'll still taste delicious!

Many Lebanese recipes call for olive oil. Olive oil adds good flavor and is low in saturated fat—the type of fat that is worse for heart health—but it is still high in calories and total fat grams. It is often a good idea to prepare the recipe as written the first time, but once you are familiar with the original you may want to experiment with reducing the amount of oil that you use. In some recipes, where oil is used to coat cookware, you can substitute a low-fat or nonfat cooking spray.

In recipes that call for butter, a common substitute is margarine. Before making this substitution, consider the recipe. If it is a dessert, it's often best to use butter. Margarine may noticeably change the taste or consistency of the food.

Meat—especially red meat—is a common source of unwanted fat. Some cooks like to replace ground beef with ground turkey to lower fat. However, since this does change the flavor, you may need to experiment a little bit to decide if you like this substitution. Buying extra-lean meats and trimming as much fat as possible is also an easy way to reduce fat. You may choose to omit meat altogether from some recipes. Replacing meat with hardy vegetables, such as potatoes or eggplant, or with meat substitutes, such as tofu or tempeh (soybean products), can keep your dishes filling and satisfying.

There are many ways to prepare meals that are good for you and still taste great. As you become a more experienced cook, try experimenting with recipes and substitutions to find the methods that work best for you.

METRIC CONVERSIONS

Cooks in the United States measure both liquid and solid ingredients using standard containers based on the 8-ounce cup and the tablespoon. These measurements are based on volume, while the metric system of measurement is based on both weight (for solids) and volume (for liquids). To convert from U.S. fluid tablespoons, ounces, quarts, and so forth to metric liters is a straightforward conversion, using the chart below. However, since solids have different weights—one cup of rice does not weigh the same as one cup of grated cheese, for example—many cooks who use the metric system have kitchen scales to weigh different ingredients. The chart below will give you a good starting point for basic conversions to the metric system.

MASS (weight)

1 ounce (oz.)	=	28.0 grams (g)
8 ounces	=	227.0 grams
1 pound (lb.) or 16 ounces	=	0.45 kilograms (kg)
2.2 pounds	=	1.0 kilogram

LIQUID VOLUME

1 teaspoon (tsp.)	=	5.0 milliliters (ml)
1 tablespoon (tbsp.)	=	15.0 milliliters
1 fluid ounce (oz.)	=	30.0 milliliters
1 cup (c.)	=	240 milliliters
1 pint (pt.)	=	480 milliliters
1 quart (qt.)	=	0.95 liters (l)
1 gallon (gal.)	=	3.80 liters

LENGTH

¼ inch (in.)	=	0.6 centimeters (cm)
½ inch	=	1.25 centimeters
1 inch	=	2.5 centimeters

TEMPERATURE

212°F	=	100°C (boiling point of water)
225°F	=	110°C
250°F	=	120°C
275°F	=	135°C
300°F	=	150°C
325°F	=	160°C
350°F	=	180°C
375°F	=	190°C
400°F	=	200°C

(To convert temperature in Fahrenheit to Celsius, subtract 32 and multiply by .56)

PAN SIZES

8-inch cake pan	=	20 x 4-centimeter cake pan
9-inch cake pan	=	23 x 3.5-centimeter cake pan
11 x 7-inch baking pan	=	28 x 18-centimeter baking pan
13 x 9-inch baking pan	=	32.5 x 23-centimeter baking pan
9 x 5-inch loaf pan	=	23 x 13-centimeter loaf pan
2-quart casserole	=	2-liter casserole

A Lebanese Table

If one word describes a Lebanese dining table, it's crowded. Meals in Lebanon are great social occasions, and the Lebanese especially love getting a big group together for mezze, or appetizers.

A buffet table of mezze is not only crowded with many people but also crowded with a vast array of dishes. Whether mezze are served at home or at a neighborhood café, they offer a feast for the senses. Dishes of all shapes, flavors, and aromas tempt hungry visitors. Diners are welcome to sample any or all of these dishes, helping themselves to tasty treats from spicy dips and spreads to fresh vegetables and salads. Mezze offerings may be as simple as nuts, olives, and cheese or as elaborate as marinated kabobs, stuffed grape leaves, and filled pastries.

One thing diners will not find on most mezze tables is silverware. Fresh, delicious breads such as the traditional flat pita are usually used to scoop up food. But whatever the dishes, and whatever the utensils, there's sure to be something for everyone on a Lebanese table.

A Lebanese family takes advantage of a sunny day to dine out on their patio.

A Lebanese Menu

Below are menu plans for a typical Lebanese lunch and dinner, along with shopping lists of the ingredients necessary to prepare these meals.* These menus are only suggestions, and as you become a more experienced cook you may enjoy experimenting with your own combinations of dishes. Remember that varying the flavors and textures of the dishes you serve will make your meals more interesting.

LUNCH

Baked kibbeh

Peasant salad

Chard and yogurt soup

Fresh fruit

SHOPPING LIST:

Produce

1 medium onion
1 cucumber
1 tomato
1 bunch or package fresh spinach
1 green pepper
3 scallions
1 head romaine lettuce
1 lb. fresh chard
1 bunch fresh parsley
1 bunch fresh mint
1 head garlic
2 lemons
assorted fresh fruit

Dairy/Egg/Meat

20 oz. plain yogurt
1 egg
1 lb. ground lamb or beef

Canned/Bottled/Boxed

1 15-oz. can chickpeas
1 small jar pine nuts
3 c. bulgur
olive oil

Miscellaneous

pita bread
salt
pepper
cayenne pepper
allspice
cumin
ground coriander
ground cinnamon
ground ginger

DINNER

Garlic chicken

Bulgur salad

Fresh fruit

SHOPPING LIST:

Produce

1 potato
1 onion
4 large tomatoes
2 small cucumbers
2 bunches scallions
1 bunch fresh parsley
1 bunch fresh mint
2 heads garlic
4 lemons
assorted fresh fruit

Meat

2 to 2½ lb. chicken pieces

Canned/Bottled/Boxed

2 c. bulgur
olive oil

Miscellaneous

salt
pepper

***If you plan to do a lot of Lebanese cooking, you may want to stock up on some of the items on these shopping lists and keep them on hand. Bulgur, garlic, and olive oil all keep well and are common ingredients in Lebanese dishes.**

Lunch / Ghadda

As in most of the Middle East, breakfasts in Lebanon are quite light. A cup of strong coffee, a piece of pita bread, and some cheese and olives are usually enough to keep one satisfied until a midmorning snack or until lunch.

Lebanese lunches are also relatively light meals. They usually consist of soup and salad, perhaps a light main dish, and fresh fruit for dessert. Many Lebanese also enjoy cups of strong, thick, black coffee flavored with cardamom seeds and often with sugar. A cup of this uniquely Lebanese coffee and a sweet snack from a street vendor or a local café are a delicious way to help ease afternoon hunger pangs.

By substituting cooked rice for meat, a host can serve these luscious stuffed tomatoes as an entrée for a vegetarian meal. (Recipe on pages 32–33.)

Stuffed Tomatoes/Banadoura Mahshi

Stuffed vegetables are very popular in Lebanon and are served as part of the mezze or as a main course.

4 large, ripe tomatoes*

½ lb. lean ground lamb or beef

¼ c. pine nuts

1 tsp. salt

¼ tsp. pepper

¼ tsp. ground ginger

½ tsp. cinnamon

¼ tsp. allspice

¼ tsp. ground cumin

1 14½-oz. can crushed tomatoes

⅔ c. water

1. Preheat oven to 350°F. Grease a 9 × 9-inch baking dish.
2. Cut tops off tomatoes. Using a spoon, carefully scoop out pulp, making sure not to tear the skins. Save tops and pulp.
3. Place tomatoes in baking dish.
4. In a large skillet, cook meat over medium-high meat until brown, stirring to break into small pieces. Remove meat from skillet with a slotted spoon and place in a medium bowl. Save the grease.
5. Add pine nuts to grease from the meat and sauté over medium-high heat 2 to 3 minutes, or until lightly browned.
6. Remove pine nuts from skillet with a slotted spoon and stir into browned meat. Add spices and mix well.
7. Place pulp from tomatoes in a fine sieve and place sieve over the bowl containing the meat mixture. With the back of a spoon, force pulp through sieve into the bowl.

8. Spoon meat mixture into hollowed-out tomatoes. Replace tops on tomatoes.
9. Pour crushed tomatoes over tops of stuffed tomatoes. Add ⅔ c. water to bottom of baking dish.
10. Bake uncovered for 20 to 30 minutes. Serve hot.

Preparation time: 35 to 45 minutes
Baking time: 20 to 30 minutes
Serves 4

*The filling used in this recipe can also be used to stuff zucchini or eggplant. For a vegetarian version, replace the meat with about 1 c. cooked rice.

Chard and Yogurt Soup/Shourabit Silq bi Laban

1 c. bulgur

1 lb. fresh chard*

8 c. water

1 15-oz. can chickpeas

1 tsp. salt

2½ c. (20 oz.) plain yogurt, at room temperature

1 egg, at room temperature

fresh or dried mint to garnish

**Any kind of greens, such as turnip, spinach, or sorrel, may be used instead of chard.*

1. Place bulgur in a colander. Rinse under cold water and drain.
2. Remove tough stems from chard. Wash leaves well and drain.
3. In a large kettle with a lid, bring 3 c. water to a boil over high heat. Add chard and return to a boil. Cover and cook about 3 minutes, or until leaves are thoroughly wilted.
4. Remove chard with a slotted spoon, place in a bowl, and set aside to cool. Save cooking water and add bulgur, chickpeas, and 5 c. more water to kettle. Return to a boil. Lower heat, cover, and simmer for 1½ hours.
5. While soup is cooking, chop chard finely with a sharp knife. In a medium bowl, beat together salt, yogurt, and egg. Add chopped chard and about 1 c. of the soup to yogurt mixture. Stir well, always stirring in the same direction to prevent curdling.
6. Remove soup from heat. Gradually add yogurt mixture, stirring constantly. Sprinkle each serving with mint and serve immediately. (Do not reheat or soup will curdle.)

Preparation time: 15 to 25 minutes
Cooking time: 2 to 2½ hours
Serves 4 to 8

Peasant Salad/*Fattoush*

Fattoush is a favorite in Lebanon and is an excellent way to use up stale pita bread. You may use any greens in this salad, such as chard, sorrel, or turnip, but they should always be finely chopped.

Dressing:

1 clove garlic

¼ tsp. salt

juice of 2 lemons (about 6 tbsp.)

½ c. olive oil*

Salad:

2 pieces stale pita bread

1 tbsp. water

1 cucumber, peeled and chopped

1 tomato, chopped

1 green pepper, seeded and chopped

3 scallions, finely chopped

¼ tsp. pepper

½ c. chopped fresh parsley

¼ c. chopped fresh mint

1 c. finely chopped fresh spinach

½ head romaine lettuce, finely chopped

1. To make dressing, crush garlic clove with a garlic press or the back of a spoon. In a small bowl, combine garlic and salt and stir to form a paste. Add lemon juice and olive oil, mix well, and set aside.
2. Place pitas on a cookie sheet and place under the broiler. Toast each side for 3 to 5 minutes, or until crisp and lightly browned. (If you don't have a broiler, cut pitas in half and toast in a regular toaster.) Break pitas into bite-sized pieces and sprinkle with 1 tbsp. water.
3. In a large bowl, toss remaining ingredients with pita. Sprinkle with dressing, toss again, and serve immediately.

Preparation time: 15 to 20 minutes
Serves 4 to 6

*To make a lighter dressing, use only ⅓ or ¼ c. olive oil and use an extra tablespoon or two of lemon juice.

Ground Lamb Mixture/Kibbeh

Kibbeh is one of Lebanon's national foods and is the basic ingredient of many dishes. Kibbeh is traditionally made from lamb that has been ground almost to a paste, but it can also be made from regular ground lamb or ground beef. This recipe makes a large amount of kibbeh. *See page 39 for a recipe that calls for this delicious staple.*

2 c. bulgur*

6 c. cold water

1 lb. lean ground lamb or beef

1 medium onion, peeled and finely chopped

1 tsp. cayenne pepper

1 tsp. salt

½ tsp. pepper

½ tsp. cinnamon

½ tsp. allspice

½ tsp. ground ginger

¼ tsp. ground coriander

¼ tsp. ground cumin

ice water

1. Place bulgur in a large bowl. Add 6 c. cold water and set aside for at least 1 hour.
2. After soaking, place bulgur in a colander and rinse under cold running water. Press bulgur between your hands to remove excess water and set aside.
3. In large bowl, mix meat and onion. Add spices and knead until mixture forms a smooth paste.
4. Put a few ice cubes in a small glass of water. Knead bulgur into meat, adding small amounts of ice water when needed to keep mixture smooth.
5. Cover and refrigerate overnight before using.

Preparation time: 1¼ hours
(plus overnight chilling)
Makes 8 portions

**Look for bulgur in the bulk foods section of your supermarket or grocery store. If they don't carry it, check at health food stores or at specialty Middle Eastern markets. You may also substitute cracked wheat for bulgur.*

Baked Kibbeh/*Kibbeh Bissanieh*

For this dish, use the basic kibbeh recipe on page 37.

1 recipe kibbeh (see recipe on page 37)

½ c. pine nuts

¼ c. olive oil

1. Preheat oven to 400°F.
2. Thoroughly grease two 9 × 13-inch baking pans.
3. In a medium bowl, stir pine nuts into kibbeh mixture, saving a few nuts for decoration. Spread mixture evenly in the baking pans.
4. Divide each pan of kibbeh into portions by scoring the top of the meat with a knife, being careful not to cut all the way through. First make four evenly spaced lengthwise cuts in each pan. Then make diagonal cuts of the same width to form diamond-shaped pieces.
5. Decorate kibbeh with pine nuts and lightly drizzle olive oil over the top.
6. Bake on bottom oven rack for 30 minutes. Then move pan to top rack and bake another 10 minutes.
7. Cut into squares or diamonds along scoring marks and serve hot or cold with salad.

Preparation time: 15 minutes
Baking time: 40 minutes
Serves 8

Fish and Rice Stew/*Sayadieh*

Sayadieh is a delicious and robust Lebanese-style fish dish. Any firm, white fish, such as haddock or cod, can be used in this recipe.

2 tbsp. vegetable oil

2 tbsp. pine nuts

6 c. water

1 onion, peeled and quartered

2 lb. fish fillets, fresh or frozen (thawed)

1 c. long-grain converted rice*

½ tsp. cumin

½ tsp. salt

juice of 1 lemon (about 3 tbsp.)

fresh parsley sprigs for garnish

1. In a small skillet, heat 1 tbsp. oil over medium-high heat. Sauté pine nuts, stirring constantly, for about 2 minutes, or until lightly browned. Remove with a slotted spoon and drain on paper towels.
2. In a large kettle, bring 6 c. water to a boil over high heat. Carefully add onion and boil 15 to 20 minutes, or until soft. Remove onion with a slotted spoon and drain in a colander. Save cooking water.
3. Place onion in a bowl and mash with a potato masher, or place in a blender and blend until onion has a pastelike consistency.
4. Add fish and onion to onion cooking water and bring water back to a boil over high heat. Reduce heat, cover pan, and simmer for about 10 to 15 minutes, or until fish is tender. Remove fish with slotted spoon. Save cooking water.
5. In a large saucepan, heat remaining 1 tbsp. of oil over medium-high heat. Add rice and cumin and cook, stirring constantly, for 3 minutes. Add salt and 2 c. of the fish cooking water. Cover pan and cook rice on

low heat about 20 minutes, or until rice is fluffy and liquid is absorbed.

6. Add lemon juice to remaining fish broth and reheat slowly over medium-high heat.

7. Arrange rice on a deep serving platter and place fish on rice. Pour hot broth over fish. Garnish with pine nuts and parsley.

Preparation time: 10 to 15 minutes
Cooking time: 1½ hours
Serves 4

**Converted rice, which is available at most supermarkets, is recommended for this recipe. However, long-grain white rice can be substituted. Converted rice is a bit darker in color than white rice and takes slightly longer to cook.*

Appetizers/Mezze

Mezze are a very important part of Lebanese cuisine. Before dinner a large selection of appetizers in tiny dishes is set out for diners. Mezze may include vegetables, kibbeh balls, savory pastries, yogurt, cheese, and olives. Lebanese restaurants compete with each other on the number of mezze dishes they offer and may serve as many as seventy!

Other dishes, especially sweets, are enjoyed as midday snacks or on special occasions. Lebanese people do not eat a lot of desserts, but honeyed pastries and candies may be eaten during the day with cups of strong black coffee or mint tea. Generally, fresh fruit or perhaps a milk-based pudding is the only dessert served after a meal.

Plunge pita bread into this eggplant dip for a winning appetizer or snack. *(Recipe on page 45.)*

Chickpea and Tahini Dip/Hummus bi Tahini

Hummus is a paste made from ground chickpeas, spices, and tahini—ground sesame seeds. This quick and simple dip is standard fare throughout the Middle East.

1 15-oz. can chickpeas

3 tbsp. tahini*

1 clove garlic, peeled

juice of 2 lemons (about 6 tbsp.)

½ tsp. salt

parsley sprigs for garnish

olive oil

1. Reserving the liquid from the chickpeas, combine chickpeas, tahini, garlic, lemon juice, and salt in a blender or food processor. Add a little of the reserved chickpea liquid and process until mixture is a smooth paste. Add more liquid if necessary.
2. Divide hummus among four small plates or serve in one dish. Garnish with parsley and sprinkle with a few drops of olive oil. Serve with pita bread.

Preparation time: 10 minutes
Serves 4

**Prepared tahini is available in Middle Eastern and Asian groceries or in the international or gourmet section of some supermarkets.*

Eggplant Dip/*Baba Ghannouj*

Eggplant dip is a favorite throughout the Middle East, where the eggplant is usually cooked over an open flame, giving the pulp a smoky flavor. Baking it directly on your oven rack will give the eggplant a similar flavor. Baba ghannouj makes a great party dip.

1 large eggplant

2 cloves garlic, peeled and crushed

1 tsp. salt

juice of 2 lemons (about 6 tbsp.)

4 tbsp. tahini

2 tbsp. water (more if needed)

4 tbsp. chopped fresh parsley for garnish

*To peel the eggplant, cut a thin slice off the top and the bottom of the vegetable. Carefully make a thin slit lengthwise down the eggplant, just barely cutting through the skin. You should now be able to peel off the rest of the skin with your fingers.

1. Preheat oven to 400°F.
2. Wash eggplant. Remove stem. Prick eggplant several times with a fork. Place directly on oven rack and bake for 30 minutes, or until very soft. Carefully remove from oven and cool.
3. When eggplant is cool enough to handle, peel off skin.* Mash it in a medium bowl with a potato masher, or place in a food processor and process until smooth but not liquid.
4. In a small bowl, crush garlic into the salt with the back of a spoon. Beat in lemon juice, tahini, and water. Stir into mashed eggplant. If baba ghannouj is too thick, add water 1 tbsp. at a time until mixture is a soft, creamy consistency.
5. Divide mixture among four small plates or serve in one dish. Garnish with parsley. Eat baba ghannouj by scooping it up with pieces of pita bread.

Preparation time: 30 minutes
Baking time: 30 minutes
Serves 4

Lebanese Pizza/*Lahma bi Ajeen*

This dish has many variations—and many names—throughout the Middle East, but it's always a favorite.

2 packages pizza dough mix (enough to make 2 12-in. pizzas)

1 recipe meat filling (see recipe for stuffed tomatoes, Steps 4 through 6, on page 32)*

2 tbsp. white wine vinegar

2 tbsp. lemon juice

¼ c. olive oil

1. Preheat oven to 450°F.

2. Prepare one package pizza dough mix according to directions on package. Divide dough into four pieces. On a floured surface, shape each piece into a ball and flatten. With a rolling pin, roll out each ball into a round about 4 inches in diameter. Repeat with second package of pizza dough. Place rounds on greased cookie sheets.

3. In a medium bowl, mix prepared meat filling with vinegar and lemon juice.

4. Spread filling over rounds of dough, leaving a narrow margin at the edge.

5. Lightly brush olive oil over the top of each pizza, coating both the filling and the uncovered edges of the dough.

6. Bake pizzas for 15 minutes, or until edges of dough are golden brown. Serve warm.

Preparation time: 45 to 55 minutes
Baking time: 15 minutes
Makes 8 pizzas

**For an easy vegetarian pizza, top with hummus (see recipe on page 44), chopped tomatoes, and sliced olives. Or experiment with other ingredients to find your favorites!*

Lemonade/*Limoonada*

Lemonade is a favorite drink in Lebanon, especially during hot weather. If you like your lemonade more or less sweet, vary the amount of sugar that you use.

2 lemons

2 tbsp. sugar

6 ice cubes

3 c. cold water

2 tsp. orange flower water (optional)*

4 slices lemon for garnish

1. If the lemons are thick skinned, cut off the two end pieces and discard. Cut each lemon into 4 to 6 pieces and place in a blender along with any juice that escaped during cutting.
2. Place lid firmly on blender and blend on maximum speed for 3 to 5 seconds.**
3. Add sugar, ice, water, and orange flower water. Blend again on high speed for 30 seconds. Pour through a sieve into a serving pitcher.
4. Serve lemonade in tall glasses with extra ice and lemon slices.

Preparation time: 5 minutes
Serves 4

*Look for orange flower water (also called orange blossom water) in the international or gourmet section of your grocery store, or check at a Middle Eastern specialty market.

**If you don't have a blender, grate the lemon peel with a zester or a fine grater and squeeze the juice from the lemon. Shake together all ingredients in a large jar, strain, and serve.

Dinner / Asha

After the mezze—if anyone is still hungry—the main dinner items are served. Dinner in Lebanon usually consists of a poultry, fish, or lamb entrée. However, a combination of several meatless dishes may be served instead. Lebanese cooking uses many grains and fresh vegetables, giving vegetarian diners a variety of delicious and authentic dishes from which to choose.

The main course is often accompanied by one or more side dishes prepared from Lebanon's staples, rice and bulgur. A large salad and a cooked vegetable dish may be included as well. After the meal, many diners enjoy coffee or tea.

Discriminating diners will appreciate the undercurrent of lemon in this baked fish with tahini. (Recipe on page 53.)

Garlic Chicken/Djaj Biltoom

4 cloves garlic, peeled and finely chopped

1 tsp. salt

juice of 1 lemon (about 3 tbsp.)

¼ c. olive oil

2 to 2½ lb. chicken pieces*

Sauce:

1 whole head garlic, cloves separated and peeled

1 tsp. salt

1 c. olive oil

2 tbsp. lemon juice

1 potato, peeled and boiled

After handling raw chicken or other poultry, always remember to wash your hands, utensils, and preparation area thoroughly with soapy hot water. Also, when checking chicken for doneness, it's a good idea to cut it open gently to make sure that the meat is white (not pink) all the way through.

1. In a large bowl, mix up a marinade of garlic, salt, lemon juice, and olive oil. Add chicken pieces and stir until they are coated. Lightly cover bowl with a cloth and refrigerate overnight.
2. Preheat oven to 375°F. Place chicken pieces in a roasting pan and discard marinade. Roast chicken for 1 hour, uncovered. Check often and drizzle olive oil lightly over chicken if it looks dry.
3. In a medium bowl, prepare sauce. Crush garlic into salt with the back of a spoon. Add 1 tbsp. olive oil and beat well. When oil has been absorbed, stir in a few drops lemon juice. Repeat until about ½ c. oil and 1 tbsp. lemon juice have been used.
4. Put garlic mixture in blender. Add remaining oil, lemon juice, and potato. Blend until mixture looks shiny and smooth. (If you don't have a blender, mash the potato, add to remaining ingredients, and beat well with a wire whisk.)
5. Place chicken pieces on a serving platter. Serve hot with small dishes of garlic sauce for dipping.

Preparation time: 40 to 45 minutes
(plus overnight marinating time)
Cooking time: 1 hour
Serves 4 to 6

Baked Fish with Tahini/Samak bi Tahini

This simple dish is usually served slightly cooled.

4 skinned fish fillets or steaks (about 2 lb.), fresh or frozen (thawed)*

salt

1½ tbsp. olive oil

Sauce:

1 clove garlic

½ tsp. salt

½ c. tahini

juice of 2 lemons (about 6 tbsp.)

fresh parsley

lemon wedges

1. Sprinkle fish with salt and refrigerate for one hour.
2. Preheat oven to 400°F.
3. Brush fish on both sides with olive oil and place in a lightly greased baking dish. Bake uncovered for 20 to 35 minutes, or until fish flakes easily with a fork and is opaque all the way through. (Cooking time will vary depending on the thickness of the fillets or steaks.)
4. While fish is baking, combine garlic, ½ tsp. salt, tahini, and lemon juice. Mix well and add water if sauce is too thick.
5. Remove fish from oven. Let cool and pour sauce over fish. Garnish with parsley and lemon wedges and serve.

Preparation time: 15 minutes
(plus 1 hour refrigerating time)
Baking time: 20 to 35 minutes
Serves 4

*Any firm white fish, such as cod, haddock, or halibut, will work for this dish.

Bulgur Salad/*Tabbouleh*

Bulgur is one of the most popular foods in Lebanon. This refreshing, flavorful salad is very typical of Lebanese cuisine.

2 c. bulgur

1 onion, peeled and finely chopped

4 large tomatoes, chopped

2 bunches scallions, finely chopped (about 1 c.)

2 small cucumbers, peeled and chopped

½ c. olive oil

juice of 2 lemons (about 6 tbsp.)

1 tsp. salt

¼ tsp. pepper

6 tbsp. chopped fresh parsley

3 tbsp. chopped fresh mint, or 1 tbsp. dried mint

1. Place bulgur in a colander and rinse under cold running water. Press bulgur between your hands to remove excess water. Return bulgur to the colander and let it drain over a bowl for 1 hour. Discard the drained water.
2. In a large mixing bowl, combine bulgur with all remaining ingredients.
3. Place mixture in a large serving bowl. Chill before serving.

Preparation time: 1¼ hours
(plus several hours chilling time)
Serves 6 to 8

Bulgur Pilaf/Burghul Bidfeen

2 c. bulgur

⅓ c. butter or margarine

1¼ c. blanched almonds, whole or halved*

1 onion, peeled and chopped

2 tsp. salt

¼ tsp. pepper

2 10¾-oz. cans (about 3 c.) vegetable, chicken, or beef broth

*Blanched almonds have been cooked very briefly to remove their skins. Look for them in your local grocery store.

1. Place bulgur in a colander and rinse under cold running water. Press between your hands to remove excess water. Set aside for 1 hour.
2. In a large saucepan, melt half of the butter over medium heat. Add almonds and sauté, stirring constantly, for about 3 minutes, or until lightly browned. Remove with a slotted spoon and drain on paper towels.
3. Add onion and sauté over medium-high heat about 3 minutes. Melt remaining butter in pan and stir in bulgur, salt, and pepper. Cook for 5 minutes, stirring frequently.
4. In another large saucepan, bring broth to a boil over high heat. Add bulgur mixture and almonds. Lower heat and cover pan tightly. Simmer for 40 minutes, or until liquid is absorbed and bulgur is fluffy and tender. If broth is absorbed before bulgur is ready, add another ¼ c. boiling broth or water and cook 10 more minutes, or until broth is absorbed.
5. Remove pan from heat and let stand, covered, for 15 minutes. Fluff pilaf with a fork and serve hot.

Preparation time: 1¼ hours
Cooking time: 1¼ to 1½ hours
Serves 4 to 6

Kabobs/Lahm Mishwi

Mishwi is one of the most common meat dishes in the Middle East. These tasty kabobs can be served as mezze or with rice and salad as a main course.

½ c. olive oil

4 cloves garlic, peeled and crushed

1 tsp. ground cumin

1 tsp. ground coriander

1 tsp. salt

½ tsp. pepper

2 lb. lamb or beef, cut into 2-inch cubes*

4 onions, peeled and quartered

2 green peppers, seeded and cut into 2-inch squares

*For lamb kabobs, leg of lamb is the best cut to use. Use lean sirloin tip or chuck steak for beef kabobs. For vegetarian kabobs, try chunks of eggplant, potatoes, or tofu.

1. In a large bowl, combine oil, garlic, and spices and mix well. Add meat to this marinade and stir until well coated. Refrigerate for at least 2 hours or overnight. If using wooden skewers, soak them in water for at least 30 minutes before using.
2. One hour before cooking, remove meat from refrigerator. Place a cube of meat onto a skewer, then add a piece of onion and a piece of green pepper. Repeat until all ingredients have been used.
3. Place skewers in a shallow broiling pan. Broil for 10 minutes, then turn over skewers and broil 10 more minutes, or until meat has browned. Carefully drizzle marinade over kabobs several times while broiling.
4. Serve hot.

Preparation time: 1 hour
(plus at least 2 hours marinating time)
Cooking time: 20 to 25 minutes
Serves 4

Cold Meat Loaf/Kafta Mahshi bil Bayd

This delicious cold entrée is good with salad and perfect for picnics—a true summer dish. In Lebanon, the meat loaf is tied with string and cooked in a Dutch oven instead of wrapped in foil. Both methods keep the loaf from falling apart while baking and produce the same delicious results.

3 eggs

1 lb. ground lamb or beef

½ tsp. cinnamon

½ tsp. zaatar*

1 onion, peeled and finely chopped

1 tsp. salt

½ tsp. pepper

½ tsp. ground cumin

3 tbsp. chopped fresh parsley

1. Preheat oven to 375°F.
2. Place eggs in a medium saucepan and cover with cold water. Place over medium heat until water boils, reduce heat, and simmer for 15 minutes. Drain water from saucepan and run cold water over eggs until they are cool. Peel cooked eggs and set aside.
3. In a medium bowl, combine meat, cinnamon, zaatar, onion, salt, pepper, and cumin. Knead thoroughly.
4. Place a strip of aluminum foil, about 14 inches long, on a clean work surface. Place meat mixture on foil.
5. Wet your hands slightly and shape mixture into a 3½ × 8-inch oblong about ½-inch thick. Sprinkle meat with parsley.
6. Arrange hard-cooked eggs end to end in the center of mixture. Shape mixture over eggs to form a loaf.

7. Wrap aluminum foil tightly around meat. Place in roasting pan and bake uncovered for 40 minutes.

8. Remove meat loaf from oven. Keeping your face away from the hot steam, carefully unwrap foil using oven mitts and a fork. Pierce loaf with a sharp knife. If juices from center are no longer pink, meat loaf is done. If not, wrap package again and return to oven for 15 minutes.

9. Leave loaf on unwrapped foil to cool. When cool, refrigerate, uncovered, until cold. Slice and serve.

Preparation time: 45 minutes
Cooking time: 40 to 55 minutes
Serves 4 to 6

*Check Middle Eastern groceries for prepared zaatar. If you can't find it, you can prepare a small amount of a good substitute by combining 2 tbsp. dried thyme, 2 tbsp. sesame seeds, and ¼ tsp. salt.

Holiday and Festival Food

A meal is an occasion every day in Lebanon, and holiday meals are even more special. The Lebanese especially love to celebrate with sweets, and many favorite dishes are desserts. Cooks prepare all kinds of pastries and sugary delicacies, and holiday guests in Lebanese homes can always look forward to a sweet treat and a cup of coffee.

Many special dishes are associated with certain religious celebrations, such as Ramadan, Christmas, and Easter. However, many Lebanese enjoy these foods during the holiday seasons, regardless of their religion. Prepare the dishes in this section to get a taste of festive Lebanon.

Filled with walnuts and cinnamon and topped with syrup, these stuffed pancakes make any meal a special occasion. (Recipe on pages 62–63.)

Stuffed Pancakes/Atayef

These delicious pancakes are sold in the souk in the winter. They are eaten by Lebanese Muslims on all festive occasions, especially during Ramadan and Eid al-Fitr.

Batter:*

1 envelope active dry yeast

1 tsp. sugar

1¼ to 2 c. warm water

1½ c. all-purpose flour

vegetable oil

Filling:

2 c. chopped walnuts

3 tbsp. sugar

2 tsp. cinnamon

Syrup:

1 c. pancake syrup or dark corn syrup

½ tbsp. orange flower water (optional)

Although the flavor and texture will not be the same, you can simplify the recipe by using any pancake batter mix instead of the yeast mixture given here.

1. Preheat oven to 375°F.
2. Dissolve yeast and sugar in ½ c. warm water. Cover lightly with a damp cloth and leave in a warm place for about 20 minutes, or until mixture begins to foam.
3. In a small bowl, prepare filling by mixing walnuts, sugar, and cinnamon. Set aside.
4. In another small bowl, combine syrup and orange flower water. Set aside.
5. Warm a large mixing bowl by rinsing with hot water and drying thoroughly. Sift flour into warmed bowl. Make a depression in the center, pour in yeast mixture, and beat into the flour. Continue beating, gradually adding the remaining warm water until mixture is the consistency of pancake batter. Cover mixture with a damp cloth and leave in a warm place for 1 hour, or until bubbly.
6. Place 1 tsp. vegetable oil in a heavy skillet and swirl to coat skillet evenly. Heat pan over high heat.

7. Pour about ¼ c. batter into heated pan. Tilt pan gently to even out batter, but keep pancake fairly thick and round. Cook until pancake begins to bubble and comes away easily from pan. Cook only one side of pancake.

8. Use a spatula to remove pancake from pan and place pancake on a greased cookie sheet or baking dish. Put 2 tbsp. walnut filling on uncooked side of pancake and fold in half. Firmly pinch edges together to keep filling in place.

9. Repeat with remaining batter and filling, adding oil to pan as needed.

10. When all pancakes are cooked and filled, place cookie sheet or baking dish in oven and bake for 10 to 15 minutes. Remove from oven and dip pancakes in syrup mixture while they are still warm. If desired, serve with sour cream or cottage cheese.

Preparation time: 1 to 1½ hours
(plus 1 hour sitting time)
Baking time: 10 to 15 minutes
Serves 4 to 6

Nut-Filled Pastries/*Maamoul*

These filled treats are a traditional Easter sweet, but they are enjoyed for many other holidays in Lebanon as well. They are also delicious when filled with ground or chopped dates.

Filling:

1 c. ground walnuts, pistachios, or almonds

⅓ c. sugar

1 tsp. melted butter

1 tsp. orange blossom water, rose water,* or cinnamon (optional)

Dough:

⅔ c. butter, melted and slightly cooled

3 tbsp. sugar

2 c. all-purpose flour

about ⅓ c. lukewarm milk

powdered sugar for sprinkling

If your grocery store doesn't carry orange blossom water or rose water, check at a Middle Eastern or Asian market.

1. Preheat oven to 350°F.
2. In a medium bowl, combine all filling ingredients and mix well.
3. To make dough, combine butter and sugar in another mixing bowl and mix well. Add flour and mix with hands. Gradually add milk. Remove dough from bowl and continue kneading on a clean work surface until dough is soft.
4. Place a walnut-sized ball of dough in the palm of your hand. Press the center of the ball to form a deep hollow. Place about 1 tsp. of filling into the hollow and pinch tightly to close. Gently roll into a ball and flatten slightly. Repeat with remaining dough and filling.
5. Place filled pastries on an ungreased cookie sheet. Bake for 15 to 25 minutes, or until bottoms are a golden brown. Remove from oven. Sprinkle with powdered sugar while still warm and allow to cool on cookie sheet.

Preparation time: 30 to 35 minutes
Baking time: 15 to 25 minutes
Makes about 2 dozen pastries

Lentil Soup/Shourabit Adas

This full-bodied soup is a traditional dish for iftar, the evening meal during Ramadan. Many ingredients—such as rice, ground lamb or beef, chickpeas, or beans—can be added to this simple soup.

1 c. red lentils, whole or split*

6 c. water

2 tbsp. olive oil

1 medium onion, chopped

salt and pepper to taste

1. Rinse and drain lentils. Place lentils and water in a large pot and bring to a boil. Reduce heat, cover, and simmer.
2. While lentils are simmering, heat olive oil in a skillet over high heat. Sauté onion in oil until golden brown. Add onions, salt, and pepper to lentils.
3. Continue simmering for 25 to 35 minutes, or until lentils are soft. Serve hot with lemon wedges and pita bread.

Preparation time: 5 minutes
Cooking time: 45 to 55 minutes
Serves 4

*Look for red lentils at health food stores and Middle Eastern markets.

Field Bean Stew/Foul Mesdames

Traditionally made during Lent, the forty-day period before Easter during which many Lebanese Christians do not eat meat, this nourishing vegetarian dish can be eaten as a main course or as an appetizer.

4 eggs

2 15-oz. cans of field beans, undrained*

2 cloves garlic, peeled and finely chopped

2 tbsp. olive oil

juice of 1 lemon (about 3 tbsp.)

1 tsp. salt

4 tbsp. chopped parsley

2 chopped scallions

lemon wedges

1. Place eggs in a medium saucepan and cover with cold water. Place over medium heat until water boils, reduce heat, and simmer for 15 minutes. Drain water from saucepan and run cold water over eggs until they are cool. Peel cooked eggs, cut into quarters, and set aside.
2. In a large saucepan, combine beans and their liquid with garlic, olive oil, lemon juice, and salt. Mix well. Simmer over medium heat, stirring occasionally, for about 10 to 15 minutes, or until heated through.
3. Pour beans into individual bowls. Garnish with hard-cooked eggs, parsley, scallions, and lemon wedges, and serve with pita bread.

Preparation and cooking time: 35 to 45 minutes
Serves 4

*Middle Eastern grocery stores and the international sections of some supermarkets sell canned Egyptian field beans especially for this dish. If you cannot get them, use canned fava, kidney, or pinto beans instead.

Festive Rice Pudding/Moghlie

Moghlie is served during many holidays and festivals in Lebanon. It is also a traditional treat to serve to visitors when a child is born. It is strongly flavored with aniseed, so you may want to use less if you do not like the taste of anise.

½ c. ground rice*

3 to 3½ c. water

½ c. sugar

½ tsp. aniseed

½ tsp. caraway seed

⅛ tsp. ground ginger

2 tbsp. chopped almonds

2 tbsp. chopped pistachios

2 tbsp. chopped walnuts

*Look for ground rice or rice flour in the baking section of your grocery store.

1. In a medium bowl, combine ground rice and ¼ c. cold water. Gradually stir in more water until mixture forms a smooth paste. Add sugar and spices and mix well.
2. In a large saucepan, bring 2½ c. water to a boil over high heat. Add ground rice mixture gradually, stirring constantly to prevent lumps from forming. Continue to stir until mixture boils again.
3. Reduce heat to low. Cover and simmer, stirring occasionally to prevent mixture from sticking to bottom of pan, for about 10 minutes, or until pudding is thick enough to coat the back of a spoon.
4. Allow pudding to cool slightly before pouring into a glass serving bowl or individual bowls. Cool to room temperature and refrigerate.
5. Before serving, sprinkle pudding with chopped nuts and serve cold.

Preparation time: 10 to 15 minutes
(plus chilling time of a few hours)
Cooking time: 25 to 30 minutes
Serves 4

Index

About the Author

Suad Amari was born in Beirut, Lebanon. She worked in the Lebanese branch of an American bank before coming to the United States with her husband in 1974. Amari misses the close-knit family life she enjoyed in Lebanon but enjoys cooking her native Lebanese cuisine and sharing it with her friends.

Photo Acknowledgments
The photographs in this book are reproduced courtesy of: © Jean Léo Dugast/Panos Pictures, pp. 2–3; © Walter and Louiseann Pietrowicz/September 8th Stock, pp. 4 (both), 5 (both), 6, 18, 30, 35, 38, 42, 47, 49, 50, 55, 60, 65, 69; © Bettmann/CORBIS, p. 10; © H. Rogers/TRIP, pp. 13, 16, 26; © AFP/CORBIS, p. 15.

Cover photos: © Walter and Louiseann Pietrowicz/September 8th Stock, front top, front bottom, spine, and back.

The illustrations on pages 7, 19, 27, 29, 31, 33, 34, 36, 37, 41, 43, 44, 45, 46, 48, 51, 52, 53, 56, 57, 59, 61, 62, 64, 66, 67, and 68 and the map on page 8 are by Tim Seeley.